THE 5-MINUTE GUIDE TO
EMOTIONAL INTELLIGENCE

THE 5-MINUTE GUIDE TO EMOTIONAL INTELLIGENCE

Your Journey Your Journal

Romi Grossberg

ISBN: 1530827442
ISBN 13: 9781530827442

Acknowledgements

First I want to thank my countless clients who had the courage to be honest, vulnerable and open to trusting themselves in my presence. To my 'Writing from the Source' and 'Creative Writing' workshop participants over the years and to all those who have tracked me down months or years later to say: "I'm still writing 5-minutes every day," you are all the reason I continue to do the work that I do and I thank you.

Thank you to the Tea Temple staff in Thailand for allowing me the space to do my work and a special thank you to Rashmi for taking a leap of faith when she first asked: "Would you like to run a one-off writing workshop?" Who knew it would turn in to years of workshops, writing therapy sessions and eventually this book.

A huge thank you to my editor and mentor Shelley Kenigsberg for your expertise, honesty and friendship. Thank you to Michael G, Sam B, Sam S, Faith H and Ross C for your invaluable feedback at different stages of my writing and editing process. Much love to my beautiful friend and artist Tia for conceptualising my front cover design and to my graphic designer at Damonza for putting it in to action.

Thank you to my two families: My Australian family across the ocean but whose love I know is always there and to my Bay family in Thailand for their endless support. A special mention goes to Bob and Tia — thank you for your undying support and for sticking by me throughout this process.

In memory of my Aunty — Sonia Bryfman
My friend, my confidant, my teacher, my conscience.

It was you who taught me the power of therapeutic writing before the words 'writing' and 'therapy' ever occurred to me in the same sentence. As a troubled teenager you were the one who had the courage to challenge me and teach me to understand and control my emotions. You taught me how to calm my muddled mind, channel my thoughts and write letters; to write the words I was unable to say.
I know you can still hear me Son. I dedicate this book to you and I know you will smile and say: "You were such a little shit of a kid and now look at you, I never doubted it."
I hope I made you proud.

Table of Contents

Introduction

Our ability to know our own true thoughts, feelings and even ourselves can get lost without a safe place to express them. It is easy to get confused in the battle between our logic-based heads and our emotion-based hearts, lose confidence to our self-critic and bow out in self-doubt. Long standing societal or family pressures can also cause us to lose direction and we can find ourselves in jobs or chasing dreams that are not really ours.

Journaling is a great way to get back in touch with the true you, to understand your thoughts, emotions, patterns and reactions to situations. In understanding yourself better, you have a greater ability to understand others.

Writing Therapy is not new but is becoming a widely recognised avenue for self-discovery and journaling in particular, is a great tool for developing and increasing Emotional Intelligence.

So, welcome to your journal and congratulations on making this first step toward getting to know yourself better through writing.

Journaling is an important part of helping you through life; helping you unload and helping remind you to celebrate the good times. This workbook will help you recognise your own state of mind and emotions and give you a greater understanding of others. Journaling aides insight in to your natural intuition which otherwise can (and often does) get interrupted by fear and an over-thinking mind. Here you will learn how to listen and trust yourself.

Journaling is a great tool for learning how to truly express yourself to your best friend – YOU! In the first few pages, we'll get you started by helping you get past procrastination, blocks or fears.

What follows is a 30-day challenge to write 5 minutes each day. Each day you will answer one prompt to help free yourself of judgment that might arise (such as, "Oh, I have no idea how to write," "This is just silly; the last time I did any writing was at high school," "I'm not the creative type," "I'm not a wordsmith," or "I don't really have anything interesting to say." You will find your voice and get comfortable in your private journal quickly. You will also learn to tap in to the natural creativity you may have forgotten you had.

This journal is your gift to you, a gift of self-love. All that I ask is that you begin with an open mind and stay honest with yourself.

It is important to keep remembering that this is FOR YOU. No judgment, no self-critic and no self-editing necessary. There is no right or wrong, good or bad. There is no particular destination. The challenge is just in the doing. So do. Write. Have fun. Get to know yourself. Express. Enjoy the process.

Getting through procrastination

L et me ask you a question, in a 24-hour day would you have 5 minutes spare? It doesn't matter if it is first thing in the morning, last thing in the evening or somewhere in between. If I asked you to write for 5 minutes every day for one month, do you think you could do it? Just 5 minutes. Good.

So the new rule is: "I sit and write for 5 minutes without interruption every day."

Now you can begin your journey through this journal using the 5-minute rule. You can always write more, in fact often you will but the 5-minute rule helps to get you there (I mean it is only 5 minutes after-all) whilst providing a level of satisfaction for achieving exactly what you set out for — 5 minutes of writing.

I wonder if this 'rule' can be applied to other areas of your life? Try the 5-minute rule to get you to the starting block for any new activity. Have you been trying to do some exercise or stretching? Been meaning to start a new project? Read a new book? The hardest part of anything is starting.

So start. Turn up. Open the first page. Stretch your hamstrings, do some sit-ups. Whatever it is, start now. It *is* only 5-minutes.

Are you a perfectionist?

In my experience as a counsellor and facilitator of *Writing From The Source* workshops, there is usually a 'fear,' 'block' or 'obstacle' that arises whenever people think about doing some writing. The very idea brings up the fear of the writing not being good enough or of not sounding smart or intelligent enough. Most students will say: "Yeah, but I am a perfectionist."

If something like this happens to you, stop for a minute and think about what that might mean. Have you ever asked yourself, what is perfection? I mean if we are all striving toward it, shouldn't we know what it is?

Let's start with some prompts. Write your answer to these questions in the space provided:

1. Have you ever read the perfect book? (I don't mean a good book, a great book, an amazing, interesting or enthralling book, I mean the perfect book!)

Can you name it?

2. Do you own the perfect outfit? Dress or suit, jeans or skirt. Is the outfit just great for that occasion or is it in itself perfect?

Do you see where I am going with this?

'Perfect' — the way we see it (or think we see it) does not really exist. It is an illusion that we can spend hours, days or years trying to achieve … and it isn't real. We can spend a lifetime feeling like unless we achieve that perfection, we have failed. Why we are striving to reach something that's not real?

So what is the definition of perfect?

Here are a few synonyms: Ideal, great, complete (umm so finish it), and accurate (check your facts). These are all achievable.

So how do we know when good is good enough? When do we press send or print or publish? What's the answer? Take 5-minutes now to write what you think.

(Notes)

Learning to listen to your body - *Gutism*

When is good, good enough? To help answer that let's get in touch with our body, more specifically our gut.

We all know the expression 'gut feeling' and this is an important part of writing. There is a school of thought that says that it is the stomach, not the brain that is the most central part of our being — the centre of our emotions.

Scientists and psychologists are now studying the gut and its relationship to our mental and emotional health and calling our stomach 'the second brain.' So why aren't we listening to it more? When you have a big decision to make in life, which part of the body do you ask? Try asking your gut. Sound a bit weird? Well let's try it. I call this an exercise in *gutism* (yes I did make up that word). I will give an example here of a question that I might face in my life. I would be asking myself to choose between two different options.

1. I am going on a holiday alone.
2. I am going on a holiday with my good friend.

Now, I want you to think of the two options that are relevant to your life. Think of a choice YOU need to make and write down your two options as clear concise sentences. They should sound like a positive fact statement, ie: I am going to...

1.
2.

The exercise:

Sit down comfortably, close your eyes and take a few breaths.

Say your first option out loud (loud - not a mumble) and then just sit, still and quiet for a minute or two. As you sit, whisper it back to yourself over and over.

Now take a deep breath and read your second option out loud and sit for a minute with this one, whispering it to yourself. Take note of your reactions — thoughts, emotions, body movements or sensations.

Did the two experiences feel different? What did your body do? Did one option make you smile? Did you smile on the inside or did your lips actually move? Did one make you feel anxious? Did your breath change? Was it shallow and tight or free and deep? Did one make you feel relaxed or uneasy?

Whatever happened, you were tuning in to your body's way of answering your question. This is your gut trying to talk to you. Write here without thinking about it or trying to work it out. Write whatever comes and don't feel you have to censor or edit yourself at all. No one is going to read this, other than you.

(Notes)

If you are still not sure about the choice you need to make, read out loud what you just wrote. Read out as if you are reading to someone else.

Can you feel the difference now? Are you surprised? Do you agree/disagree? Is your logical mind trying to get involved and argue?

What this exercise is doing is helping you tune in to your gut; it's allowing you to practice listening to your gut. Breathe, listen and write. My advice is to practice reading out loud what you've written. When you read, do it with expression and intonation. By the time you have finished reading it out loud (and, often, even before then), you'll know what your gut is telling you.

Your body will sigh and smile and then you'll know there's agreement. Or your stomach will cringe and churn and you will have your answer.

I will give you an extreme example of *gutism* from my personal experience.

In 2013 I was living in Phnom Penh Cambodia and had finished a long work contract. I was at a crossroads and had no strong idea of what to do next.

I wrote a list. I was on my second stage of three different interviews for exciting, high-calibre jobs and so my list was four columns and for each job I listed the pros and cons; the positives and negatives. Now I do love my lists and in this case, 'other' was the fourth column.

In Jobs 1, 2 and 3 I wrote long lists of pros and, as appropriate, the cons though for each, there were fewer negatives than positives. Then, in the fourth column I wrote 'move to Thailand and write a book'. This option also included having no income. No support. No guarantee of anything. So, it was ridiculous, right? Then I added one thing to that column. It was the statement — 'because I want to'.

My logical mind told me I was being irresponsible and childish and that I couldn't just go and do something because I wanted to. I sat with my heavily lopsided list and started to read it all out loud. There was a lot of pride and prestige in the jobs but when I read my fourth option, my whole body smiled. At that moment, I just knew.

As I write this now, I am sitting on the balcony of my bungalow in the jungle looking over the beach in south Thailand.

Do you have something interesting to say?

Another comment brought up frequently at my writing workshops is: "I don't have anything interesting to say, it has all been said, why is my opinion interesting or different."

What I have come to know, through the many hours I have spent with writers and those learning to write is there, truly, is ALWAYS something interesting to say. And I know, for certain, it is something you will quickly learn going through your new journal.

The question of why your opinion is different or relevant can be answered very easily. You are you and no one sees the world the way you do.

If, for example, you and three of your friends went to the same bar together, drank the same drink and participated in the same conversation, your account of the evening would be four separate stories. Of course, there would be common elements but if it were a truly personal rendition of the night, you would have four different accounts of the exact same scenario. Those accounts would depend on how you were feeling that night, what was going through your mind and how you perceived each conversation.

So, the thing to remember when you start is that your opinion is always unique and different. (Maybe you want to go out with friends and try this experiment?)

Journaling is only for the
depressed or introverts

Let's debunk this myth immediately!

Unfortunately many people think that journaling is only useful to get us through dark, heavy moments, to document our feelings during break-ups or illnesses or loss of jobs and income; in fact for any perceived failures. And it's true that writing when you are going through a hard time can be very useful. Many people write only when life is pretty hard.

But I would ask that you always remember to take note of the good moments, the smiles, the tears of laughter, the first kisses and the highs of life. In this journal you will do both.

Whether you are an introvert or extravert, socially awkward or the life of the party, journaling is useful. Journaling can help you understand yourself in a way that just sitting and thinking or talking to a friend cannot. You can be completely honest and vulnerable in your journal. It will reflect back to you without opinion or judgement.

So, hopefully we have begun to chip away at some old habits around doubt, perfectionism and procrastination. We've started learning how to listen to our body and are becoming a little more confident at finding our voice.

Now I'm offering you a challenge. All you need to remember is that for the next 30 days, you will open this journal and write for 5 minutes every time. It is only 5 minutes and in 30 days you will have learnt a whole lot about yourself, your thoughts and emotions and realise the creativity you have within.

Remember that this is YOUR journal. You can read and write from front to back or close your eyes, open on a random page and start. Each prompt has space for writing and there are spare pages at the back.

There is no right or wrong. It is all just as it is meant to be. So have fun, let go, be honest with yourself and enjoy it.

Write how you feel right now about what you have read so far and about embarking on this new journal journey of self and life discovery.

Did you learn something new or did it reinforce something you already knew? Are you excited, nervous or indifferent to continue?

Think about something that made you smile this week. How did that make you feel? Where did you feel it? Was it a 'lip smile' or a full body experience? Did you sense it in your eyes, your breath, your mind? What did you do? Did it make you want to hug someone? Jump for joy? Or was it more of a quiet smile to yourself?

Close your eyes and picture that moment — that smile, that breath, your eyes, your body, your insides. Sit with that for a moment. Feel it.

Open your eyes and write about it. No judgments, no thinking, no self-editing. Just write.

(Notes)

What was the last adventure you went on? Where did you go? What did you do? Who did you do it with? What was the highlight? Write for 5 minutes about any aspect. (If you can't remember, maybe it is time you went on one).

(Notes)

L ook around the room and pick an object, any object (or pick an object from nature if you have a garden, a balcony or a window near by). Have a good look at it. Look at its colour, texture and the feeling it evokes. Is it old and dusty, cracked, shiny, brittle, smooth, bright, dull etc.

Now let's turn this object in to a person. We are going to give it personality, character and an action.

Remembering the qualities you just noted, does this object feel to you old or young? (How old, how young?) Does it feel male or female? What would a male/female at that age with those qualities be doing at this point in their life?

You can write it from the first (I, me) or third (he, she) person perspective, or better yet, give him/her a name (e.g.: John was walking down the street...).

Don't overthink it. There is no right or wrong. There is no good or bad. There is no finishing line or destination to reach. It is just a story. Let the creative part of you shine through. Without another thought — go!

(Notes)

When was the last time you spoke to a stranger?

Write about what happened. How did it make you feel? What did you say and do? What was their reaction? (Would you do it again?)

Write here for 5-minutes.

(Notes)

Think about something that made you frustrated this week. Think for a moment how it made you feel. Was it a quiet frustration confined to your mind? Did your face tense up? Did it travel to your body?

Close your eyes and picture that moment — that frustration, your breath, your face, your body, your insides. Sit with that for a minute.

Open your eyes and write about it. No judgments, no thinking, no self-editing. Just write.

(Notes)

How did it feel to write about a frustration that you had on Day 5 of this journal? In writing how you felt, did you feel you also understood the frustration or know better how it affected your body and mind? Let's try and get to the bottom of it over the next couple of pages, shall we?

In one paragraph, being as straight to the point as you can, what were you actually frustrated about?

Look at what you just wrote and ask yourself this — what is that *really* about? And write your answer.

Look at the last thing you wrote and ask yourself again — what is that *really* about? And write your answer.

Look at what you just wrote and ask yourself again — what is that *really* about? And write your answer.

Keep going until you have that 'aha' moment and understand for yourself what it was *really* about. Sometimes when we are upset, annoyed or frustrated, the reason for the response can be hidden and it may also not be what we think it is. By asking yourself what it is really about in different ways, you can delve deeper in to what is behind it.

If using the question: 'What is it really about?' doesn't resonate with you, try enquiring by simply asking 'Why?' or 'and then.'

Close your eyes and take three long deep breaths before reading on. Stop right here and close your eyes now for three breaths and then open them.

Without thinking about it, what is the first word that comes to your mind? Absolute first word.

Now straight away write here for 5 minutes using that word as your inspiration. Don't think about it, there is nothing to think about. Go.

(Notes)

Now let's have some fun. Do you remember your first kiss? Your real first kiss that made you wobble at the knees. Write the story of your first kiss as if it is in a romantic novel. Without judgment. Just enjoy it.

(Notes)

Ever played the game 'If you were an animal'? It's a fun way to open your imagination, find your inner strengths and vulnerabilities.

If you *were* an animal, what would you be? It may be that you instantly come up with the more common animals: dog, cat, or even go wilder and pick elephant or giraffe. Take the time to think outside the box and away from your mainstream. Describe here what you, as that animal, could be doing. Have fun.

(Notes)

Now that you've had some practice in writing and letting go of judgment, let's try something that you may (or may not) find a little more difficult. Are you up for it?

Write your 'inner child' a letter. By that I mean your five or six year-old self, ten if you want to. Try and remember what you dreamt of being back then. Was it a serious dream or an 'I want to be an astronaut or ballet dancer' child-like dream (although of course some people did do that). What kind of child were you? Look at what you are doing now. Do you have the same habits or patterns?

It can be a giving-advice-style letter or anything you choose. You can tell yourself to be brave, to be humble, to be more outgoing, to be yourself or that you are beautiful already. You can tell yourself that everything will be all right. Write whatever you want. Write from your heart.

Dear .... (your name)

(Notes)

What was the highlight of this week? Write what it was (it can be big or small, the first one that comes to you) and tell us about it. Why was it a highlight? How did it make you feel? What did it make you do (if anything)? Did you remember to celebrate it?

(Notes)

What was the lowlight of this week? Write what it was (it can be big or small, the first one that comes to you) and tell us about it. Why was it your lowlight? How did it make you feel? What did it make you do (if anything)?

(Notes)

What was the most significant thing you learnt this week? It can be something vital to your work, home life or about you as a person. What if anything, will you do differently now knowing what you know? Write about its impact on you, for 5 minutes.

(Notes)

What was the last dream that you remember? Write what happened. If you only remember snippets, then fill in the rest with your imagination. What do you think it meant?

(Notes)

Think of the last time you sat with a friend (or group of friends) and had a good old-fashioned 'talk the night away' ... you know the eating bad food, maybe a beer or glass of wine, sitting around on the couch til late kind of night.

Write about it — set the scene; Who was there? How did you end up there? Where were you sitting? How did the conversation begin and end? Was it fun and funny or deep and moving? Write whatever you want about it.

(Notes)

CONGRATULATIONS!

You are officially halfway through your journal 30-day challenge.

Did you know your were this amazing, interesting, insightful and creative?

Take a moment to reflect on your responses so far. Think about how you are feeling and what you have learnt about yourself.
    Which prompts have you found most:

Fun?

Challenging?

Insightful?

Creative?

Are you ready to keep going?
    Let's go.

What was the last book you read (or movie)? Can you re-write the ending? Try it here.

(Notes)

Ever wanted to say something to someone but didn't have the courage? Any missed opportunities? Any thing like the moment he/she was moving to another country or about to walk down the aisle and you wished you had the courage to say ....

Have you had a good friend hurt you and you wished you had the courage to say ....

Any boss promote someone else when you knew something that should change that decision and you wished you had the courage to say....

Now is your chance to get it off your chest.

Tell them, right here, right now. Be brave. Be bold.

(Notes)

You are all dressed up in your favourite outfit, looking fabulous and feeling sexy. You are on the way to the most exciting party full of all your favourite people waiting for you. Write a story about it. Describe what you are wearing. Describe your entrance. Who do you go up to first? What do you say? What do you do next? How does the night end?

(Notes)

Remember the last time you cried? A good tears-rolling-down-your-cheeks, sobbing cry. Write what happened when you felt that. What was going on for you?

(Notes)

Now we are going to write a different 'inner child' a letter. By that I mean your 12 or 14 year-old self. If you prefer, write to your 16-year-old self.

What kind of teenager were you? Were you rebellious? Loud and obnoxious? Flirty? Shy? Pimple faced? Tall? Short? I was a tall, too confident flirt at school and a rebellious nightmare at home. (Sorry mum and dad).

Look at how you behave now; what you're doing now. Do you have the same habits or patterns? It can be an 'if I knew then what I know now' style letter or anything you choose.

You can tell yourself to be brave, to be humble, to be more outgoing, to be yourself or that you are beautiful already. You can tell yourself that everything will be all right. Write whatever you want. Write from your heart.

Dear …. (your name)

(Notes)

You have been writing in full sentences for a while now so let's take a short break from them for this day's writing.

Now, I love lists. Do you? Try one here.

Make two columns on the next page and, in Column 1 jot down what you have learned from experience that you **want** or need in a partner.

In Column 2 put what you have learned from experience that you **don't want** in a partner. Be specific.

Make sure at the end you 'pretty up' column 1 with colours and smiles to remind you this is the list you desire.

Read this list (the colourful one) out loud and let it sink in.

(Notes)

Since you have already written a list on the page before it would be a shame not to utilise it, don't you think?

Describe the ideal partner (they may be in the next room or still only in your head). Describe them physically, mentally and emotionally. Envisage what profession they would have, what habits, hobbies, likes and dislikes. How would they treat you, talk to you, look at you.

Write for 5-minutes who this person is. Let's see if we can manifest them in to your life. Be as detailed as you can and invite them in.

If they exist for you already, maybe you can use this space to write them a love letter.

(Notes)

Think of a recent family catch up, it could have been with a sibling, parent or partner. Pick one of the conversations or outings you had (in the kitchen, in the car, at a café, a park) where there was a misunderstanding, a communication breakdown or an argument. Who was it with? One person or a few?

See if you can write this scenario from the perspective of the others involved — as if they were telling the story.

This is not always an easy exercise, but it is an important one in learning to let go of 'being right'. You may get to the end and realise maybe they had a point, or they were hurting too, or you may feel your argument is valid even still. Either way you will have inevitably gained insight in to the dynamics of the misunderstanding.

(Notes)

Day 24

Think about something that really annoyed you lately in your professional life — at work or study, something that pissed you off. Now write about it — I mean really get it off your chest. Completely. Write until you have that 'Aah that's better' kind of feeling.

(Notes)

Remember the last time you laughed - a good tears-in-your-eyes belly laugh. Write what it was about. How did your body respond? Which parts did what? Writing about it should make you laugh all over again.

(Notes)

So far you have written a letter to 'little you' and 'medium-sized you', now let's write a letter to the future you.

Without any instruction, just write whatever it is you feel like writing to your future self.

Dear ... (your name)

(Notes)

A re you ready to try on a different voice?
Pick a theme or style of writing that you would not ordinarily do. If you have an imaginative fiction style of mind, try and write something non-fiction and based in fact. If you normally like to read or watch thrillers, change tack and try to write a romantic or children's story. (My friend once challenged me to write my first sex scene – it was super fun and incredibly revealing on how I thought about sex).

Don't overthink it. Just try it. Enjoy the process.

(Notes)

Day 28

On Day 24 I asked you to think of something that really annoyed you in your *professional* life. Today I'd like you to recall something that really annoyed you in your *personal* life, something that pissed you off.

Now write about it – I mean really get it off your chest. Completely. Until you have that 'Aah that's better' kind of feeling.

(Notes)

What kinds of things make you smile? Thinking about it now should make you smile. Describe how it feels to smile as if you are telling someone who has never seen or experienced a smile. Visualise it. Feel it. What does this feeling compare to? Be as descriptive as you can.

(Notes)

This is the last day of your challenge; your last entry in this journal. You ready?

Write yourself a love letter. Write the most beautiful, amazing, delicious love letter you have ever written — and yes it is to you, how incredible!

Dear ….. (your name)

(Notes)

5 minutes a day, 30 days down… I knew you could do it. Congratulations!

Did the 5-minute rule make all the difference in getting you to write? Did procrastination creep back in? Maybe you even walked away from the challenge for a while … Either way, you are here. You made it. Well done.

Did the creative prompts such as Days 3, 9, 16 and 18 get your creative juices flowing? Did they remind you that you have a natural gift or was it difficult to tap in to? What about the prompts looking at frustrations or arguments such as on Days 5, 6 and 23? Were you fully able to let go and get to the bottom of your own thinking patterns? Could you see more clearly how you process these types of emotions? Did you discover where in your body you hold them? Were you able to do the same for the more positive prompts about smiles and laughter on Days 1, 25 and 29? Could you recreate those emotions and discover where in your body you hold and express them? I trust you smiled as you remembered and wrote.

I hope you found your writing flow and discovered a new found confidence in your voice and ability to express your truth. I trust this journal brought new clarity around your emotions, the way you think, digest and understand yourself and others.

I hope this journal helped you reconnect to your intuition and taught you how to lessen the interruptions from fear and an over-thinking mind so you could begin to listen and trust yourself. These are all tools for increasing Emotional Intelligence. Whether you found the exercises easy or difficult, you will have developed a greater understanding of yourself and in turn, of others.

I should also thank you for indulging me and sharing in the birth of my new word 'gutism' — such a goodie, I just had to use it. Maybe this exercise will become your 'go-to' when needing to make decisions in life?

The letter writing prompts deserve special mention as many people find this the most challenging — writing to yourself at different ages and stages of life. I hope you enjoyed this challenge and were fully able to open yourself to it, particularly the love letter at the end. What a beautiful gift to yourself. I hope you write this kind of letter more than once in your life. Maybe it is time to make a deal to write yourself a love letter once a year.

Maybe every New Year? Even mail it to yourself so the first thing that happens every January from now on is that you receive a love letter from your best friend — YOU! Start each year with a smile.

Please feel free to send me a message. I would truly love to hear how it went for you, whether you found it difficult, easy, helpful etc. If you have any thoughts, feelings or questions, I will gladly respond. www.romigrossberg. com

You can fill these blank pages with thoughts on your 30-day writing challenge. How did this journal experience go for you? Which ones were challenging? Easy? Fun? Which ones surprised you? Did you love it? Hate it? Or just endure it? Do you want to start it all over again (you can if you like) or buy one for a friend who you think could benefit from it also?

Here are a few pages to write your final thoughts ... but don't stop then ... **when the paper runs out, just keep writing!**

(Notes)

(Notes)

(Notes)

(Notes)

(Notes)

(Notes)

(Notes)

(Notes)

(Notes)

(Notes)

(Notes)

16903172R00055

Made in the USA
Middletown, DE
03 December 2018